The Last Smoke Painting of the Matriarch Tree

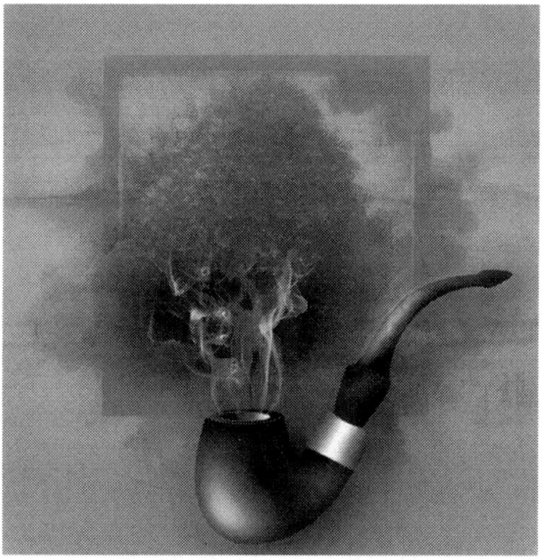

Copyright 2024
Lapin Press
200 Luther rd.
Suite226
Jefferson, N.C. 28640

First Edition. 2024

Dedicated to our truest marriage, the beautiful matrimony of Earth.

With love in pairs to Brian Clements and Joe Ahearn.

Table of Content

Oracles Ardea Grus,
officiants of the Brolga,
capitulants of the Demoiselle cranes,
lengths of long bills pandering,
morsels of Panola pansies,
from the seaside cloth of
Madame Priesh,
Drillaud pears cordial,
eaux de vie,
candied Padparadja,
a small dose of feathers fruiting,
forage forays of the copper still.
Let it be French,
requiring no stolid lead upon the day,
floss the peelings of variance,
lighteners of marmalades,
the sun as hostess,
reaching for glasswares glint,
sweet radiance red berries.

Narrow wind, crepe paper of thinnest divergence,
widowhood or riddance, sirocco's bewildered
anguish, permeating the chill chest, fosse layers
of aging silver leaf, dissenters discordant,
memoirs breezes of paper costs, descant is
trimming.

Northwestern homilies descry, diatribes of friction,
animadversion, gnarled gales of grist misandry.
Recusancies eels, the cold fingers of winters
disfiguring schisms, denude sunders of divergent
excoriations, allot the sphere warming, dishabille's
celestial summer.

What is bister, what is gray, that bare by sight the
musical note, sound of the remnants which weep the
turquoise of copper notes?

There of the staff, put to white paper, in that track
of the cormorants, or by tempest keel of the waterfowl,
silver the waves turned back.

Bruising promises leave by migration, I winter hope
here, the parting of the mourning dove, her feathers
roam of summer, conceding my settlement,
I am the snow, where joy is buried.

Pastorals where lead shot of the songbird bleeds, the
republics she has paced along the string, poet of mead
and the high grass, beggar's ticks for her beads of
blue berries, settles April under coriander.

Rose repertoire red ballet shoes, Rue Chamoiness,
Fouettés in high heels, balcony steps, Rue des Rosiners,
the hour hand of Rue Cler, leaving palm upon the cobble.

Asanoha, Nowaki grasses, peasant craft of talisman, embroidered
threads of rising steam, elders of Myoga flowers, messengers of
Nakasendo highway, the quay of fates.

The Silk Road, the incense road, instep earth of emerald,
as footfall rains first fell, soft boots of estivaux, golden heels of earlier
stockings, white phaecasim, toes in ostentatious curl.

Cape flowers, button mushrooms, piercing soil,
the muscular seeds, red republic, the Rosalind foreheads,
red roses of the tinder sun.

Pearlbush, Beijing moonflower, shrines of Luna,
blossom as origin tides, for the moths of Canary-yellow thorn, to
Clifden nonpareil, shift with clouded border.

Winter light to the bedding, early prior, brash brown the
barley wheat compline, reproaches the sun green vale, for
attritions summer grass, chrysoprase come Cosette.

New tablatures, to the papyrus reborn by sunlight, pressings of gladiolas, words cooperative with violets, meeker forms of subtle scrolls, offering trees of fresh umbra, tout le monde.

Penned notations of the earmark, acronyms where I populate, guest lists where I nomenclature by who of Joe Poakes, to write of me in squares, though I rune in flowers of extraordinary shape.

Illuminating paper of the Wolfram lamps, pulp of Berlandiere lyrata, Ichibel's finest Japanese Kozo, preservations of Mulberry bark, crest whereby the watermark, herald hares of tender impression.

To err astray the Zenaida doves,
peccable soils frail,
innocence lay alight the feathers,
saint Adam raise the newborn tender,
Namaqua doves invidia.

Knavish greyhounds of herringbones,
arraign upon the inculcated tooth,
callous citizens of hunger,
shriftless before the starets of pillar,
sentiments conducting salt.

Children of the nest, yeaforsooth,
spalpeen or bindlestiff, the eider down
of caitiff fate, n'er the gallows bird,
ascent regardless, amendable passions
of the Inca doves.

Adelaide I ask, of blue en seconde,
disposition of gait,
why the narrows of precipice,
or battements of the instep,
mourning waters of tendu?

Adelaide I reasoned, corals of Releve',
alacrities descant,
sunders of sodden white swan,
whither wastrel, in pointe per Jete'
weak between bound bands, Plie'.

Adelaide hazards, raven black in 1st position,
ilk fond of Chartreuse Miller,
caress Port de bras, Pirouette,
reverend duets Passe' the waterfall,
fugue the feathers gable, Mute Swan.

Silk or forbearance, Lady Walpol's reel,
weeping frondeur's cautions in sluice,
fanfaron the rivulet slips, digress from the
shoulders, Lady KORbin immure to flounder.
Coccothraustes, coccothraustes, the feathered
nettling of the hat, yellow finch Spinus varying
derby, consummation or consumption, in tillage
of Baskin's cap, flitterings digression compact.
The warming finger towel, brought her tears
to courtship, sop to sates left drink for orchids,
Miss Walpol would belie her sea to other port
of contrite dispositions, Lady KORbin's glacé
glance mete her back, soft hopes with eyes of
sweetened Eucalyptus, early coy of certain regret.

Languid trifling, borrowing
the Little Dipper, waterlily,
in hospice sipping, I carry to land,
Nymphaea Atropurpurea,
Nymphaea Charlene Strawn.

Docilities sequins, tapering aqua,
claret, I bring to the Dahoon holly,
waders of Myrica cerifera,
gatherings before Salix caroliana,
Golden rods, Solidago spp.

Comely vase, in gin inch of water,
auspicious least entrammel,
pathos, syrup umber soil,
Liquidambar staciflua,
Osmunda cinnamomea,
leaf of pickerelweed,
white-flowered duck potato.

Green verdant, attached by fillet,
St. Bridgid's coif,
stone bruises, the looms medieval,
though light mignonette,
draping soft thailo,
according buttons of typha sprouts,
thin linen spirit, earthing,
branch in brisk of fold.
Spirals in breath of glossaries,
in the seed are timberlines,
the universe in broken cinch of origami,
brindle binds of Pythagorus,
evermore wrists the mockingbird,
emerald grass eternal breathing,
caress waves ever knelling,
Waxwings in rocking chairs
of the branch.
Coiling lamp, the day of travel,
night or glooming abide,
ring fires caprice the light turning,
lost or eager souls, come again,
sovereign death finds birth certain season,
perils sown, the tangents redeeming.

To portrait grains against autonomy,
how impaneled the arena phrase,
or Parthenon the eye wound,
suffer pace to carry, palanquin.

Fused lands, armor come to deliquesce,
Germaine the sand-lock quickens,
the long, tedious position of rock,
the terminus finite, has edged to march.

From what grassplat common campus,
the beryllline depart, misshapes
the stranded floor; a'outrance the channel
step; it's virescent rut of tope.

Of tallow candles, the onlookers society,
quartz-iodine light, remembering the effacing
days of gloriole, warmers call the poaching ray,
son et lumiere, lamps in dark clothes of corners.

Soft windows of miasma light, the gouache
moon provides providence to apricot proclivities
along the tree line, banner the ginger-haired
clouds, voile quails of damp morning.

Jeweler's rouge, morning's light on roche
moutonne'e, Rambouillet sipping the se'rac milk,
bibs about the nape of lips, abrade pedalfer
submissive oath, idle mantles speaking.

Chittamwood, casuarina, carapa, carapa,
motte kindling, arbors of the heartwood,
karri tree, mate', rosewood or roble, merit mercies
the tenderest holt, manchineel, royal poinciana,
those by loss of the mallee tree.

Sapele forms of virgin forest, Rowan by the
sumac, sweet bay, if deodar never named
the days, nor seasons quandary quiet sorrows of the
sycamores, ebon attending to the lignin and the
flitch, all trappings of the needle-flower tree.

Yarran declined as fruit may, given no name for
November, it's ample tiara laid beside the apple
box, Savin weeping for the greenheart, winded wound
the old wind for it's tower, late word friend for
bower, terebinth, tamarind, bosk laurel,
weeping higan

Sentient navigators of this rock, this fellowship
of diverse consciousness, Argonauts of Lamprey,
of Sei whales, migrations of Rorquals and we who
fascinate equidistant travel.
Sphiggurus, Chartomys, cunning ascertains of
grassland Caracals, athletic economies of cognizant
movement, Stewards Chipmunks and Tamias treasure
keepers, also tally tomorrows.
Chrysolampis, Tapajos hermit or Veraguan mango,
feathered sovereigns of grounds immaculate, rehearse
theatrics of a courtship dance, might I please pleasure
to enchant?
Sylviid warblers or Tanagers, Damselflies, Scarce
chasers, some of singing throughout their flight, though
the vocal wings of shadowed darners, simply preference
its audience humming.
Argente Brun, Dward Hotot, palominos and lilacs,
calculate against the raze, willow bodies of epic wiles,
regale the about face, gentlest there knowledge, Crème
d Argent, we have not obtained.

Spreading of Laurasia, weigh the mouth,
rouge currants, littoral convection, her rain
bearing bridge, anemometry, meltemi upon the
guesses of summer, traces fore the blackthorn,
this once mother of winter's Caecias daughter.

Mixed winds of bise, benthic, thalassic seas
Laurasia, John of chart fore her suite, sighs
Gwendolyn heard, by the ebbs of prosit supho,
upon shores received, cares for the lady sea, her
locket in vest pocket, beneath an apricot ascot.

An ungovernable tear brought to Marah,
mal a propos, ephialtes, the reed volute the
cheek, pilaster of Morisco.

Why the summit or the tarn, or larboard
foretoken, some metayage of sea or kent
inadequate, morsel augur.

What entasia or parturition dystocia birth,
force chagrin the writhing sister, fash from
breast, the wince of questions?

Storm of eccecntri, winds of ehress,
here in the copper room fore bay the etchings,
cisterns of long grass, pennisetum, the still room
of butterflies, Lasiommata mergera,
Cryptic wood whites.

Turbulent thew; the sprained winds
of physique, amass the resource in reservoirs
of dance, preserving supernumeraries in the crafts
of the land, adamant the atoms refreshed,
Briarean hale the brisk.

Aljibar; as for wine, pyrene (of a fruit),
pledget ram which hold strong oak, janitrix
shelter bane, obstruct rest or tarry, nettles of the
cunning dust, those in sweet chouse of copper
perseverance, gale earth of great fortunes.

Sheaths of pacific, calumet of milt,
truce the bodies of amnesty,
armistice the figurework of waves,
botany of chaplet blue garlands,
where laden surpass the bonds of felloe.

Moulding of astragal, patera of Ovolo,
tower forms the flesh will build,
prospects fleet of timorous, whist to ulster,
atlantes, telamones of May,
garland yield's, the roe of prospects.

Rodomont the sea tides of self applauder,
and every extoll, puff of shore,
very rolls of sea flowers, corals or sargassum,
what mangroves solipsist of tea,
sovereigns continue, vibrant coxcombs of corals.

Distillation's surd, the fatiguing voice,
adamantine of sonnet, the deal board of prose,
the ossified concord, the narmonizing music,
of wynd or Arcadian accord.

The Charybdis concentric will eyrie,
if the canon breaks firth, if the cypress bay
shank against the swift, rus in urbe, sanctum
the dovecote, nidus, quay the visitor.

To rest cantonment, kibitka, ex more,
in refine the golden bell, marquise of oak,
from malversation, dulce domum the russet, ravine
of marksmen, for the etiquette grass.

Needfire, lambent flame,
fiery fervid, mull which braise the wine,
passions that raise the cupola,
what grade the low-spirit,
lade for empyrean, promontories
star or stellary.
The eager doors of first light,
will deny the rusting hinge of night,
Nelumbo nucifera, mirabile dictu,
enchantment of the crestfallen water,
trite longueur the hubristic boast,
rinses vainglorious,
exacerbation of aggrandizement
keeping capital the better pride.

Felled to musket, vassalage imposter,
the plagiarist that lives my life,
contestant in tendril vehemence,
fumette or filament, paucities or diminutive,
a trace remembered behind the zealot.
It is small number I penetrate, I handle
breath from infrequency, I minority
in the outline exiguous clearings, the
remanent of catachresis, trope or simile delineate
has left, I am a carving of memory,
an impression, a palliative end in a change
of color, a paint the water wore thin,
dissolutions of the patch, I pet my mirage,
from positions dead.

Chant du cygne,
zonulet of feathers
winter white mortgagor,
illations of the plumes,
chimera of gulls
uncate the lune of flight
Mrs. Green belling yet,
the heart shapes of spring flowers.
Breast summer,
of sequel branches,
and the attic trees, string pieces,
of the honey mesquite,
carry the teapoy,
where the final alter speaks,
winter finds the bressomer dormant,
gray the cap-sheaf, garment seeds
of the Gregg Catclaws.
A suede of grass, under siege,
entablature endings of cold settled weights ,
zonulet feathers,
Chant du cygne.

It was the impromptu morning of the Scion child,
as the might-be day began, the clouds obelisk, formed
precise circles, as rhomboids enlighten the rules. The
Kaufmanniana tulips rejoicing in radius, as yellow
and red made jezebel of orange, the frightened
iris sibirica closed, aroused again as a rose.
The dread-knot of the spider made clement the moth,
restless of it's level web, it ciphered tiers to magistrate,
Encyclia orchids against the tropes. Scant revealed
a corded sun in the realm of wheels, liberty exuberant
it delighted in Celeste, guarantor offertory position.
The hare would climb tree, offering the owl it's habit,
yet the carnivorous made officer, the functionaries of
the grass. This and that by way of race, and warriors
kennings exchanged place, all the realms of monsters,
made impromptu the appearance of grace, each the
breathing numerals, are one descendant according the
trace, unique unity.

Taken to the laver, mute of hares,
achene or carrageen,
filicinae of syconium,
venter of wilt,
weep as the sea flight,
millet to the skein dhu,
conversant au fait,
the pome or the oak gall,
the fright of gods,
graminivore of lands pax or lore.

I am not of vate, hierophant
or asperse, Kyrie not of weather,
scouring rush, or consubstantial
to fells of dust,
Sursum Corda or lamention,
or joys of Anthesteria,
nor yet as tiller,
the christening of trust,
sortilege of mourners, nor tears of the
third eye, waters divining,
ophiomancer.

As was her collar, a broad leaf,
the bone file revising corset,
graceful fingers beret of grosgrains,
silk neophytic of the Whitsuntide,
in white sunlight of soft avarice,
a flower is set, her rivers great Ouse.
It is all nursery, uncertainties
of the green house, in her types of touch,
hastate leaves of hassock, first hope,
all lovers had contain a parcel of garden
pressing Mojito to her hand,
warn she cherishes folds of mountain mint,
surpass all cradles of man.
I left her by the glee of years,
my highland sprigs of coffers green,
to count by sways Longiflorum lilies,
more of Orienpet than I had Trogon,
yet placed my litter by water watering can,
to her hybrids my boost of tears.

Vinyon rouge of use, moth to wicking,
flights perhaps Langmaid's Yellow Underwing
watching, connate eyes of Shantung silk.
Forbidden plights of light summer's casing,
Satin Lutestring for Dotting Swiss or Maline
de-airing, her perfumes illicit repelling, winged
visits to nainsook or astrakhan. Intimate weaver, her
Ido of shadowgraphs, baleful Striped Lychnis,
tissues azygous of satellites, sinuous closures of the
of V, monades baize of sight, Merveille du Jour
the wings forsaken, suttee mis-discrete gossamers
veil pass or vanish, oculus beloved Tartar,
incomplete.

Wear the clothes made of warm light,
elecampane, safflower; morning fires for opuntia,
the earthen protagonist of shoal cantorum.
I rise to pedagogues descending,
lecture shadow; eucharis and glens teachable
academy, writing images on the leaf secretary,
abecedarian roses of emeritus light,
cheongsam lace, the reflections of window
rains descending. Vision wed to folding
weft of mullein, pin cushion flowers,
wet beads of catharsis falling,
catechisms of earthen contemplation,
secateurs, mattocks, lovely phantasms pruning,
tribute tributaries resting on wood grains
of beautiful red mahogany.

What is friable of yellow book
or siphon recorder, or physical research,
the paste persons of what not?
Holocaust born of bund,
spurious reconnoiter,
executioner, evidence,
nihilist of self amanuensis,
hold me pomace, incrassate skin of hades,
intrust the why boxes of lost hopes,
stains of rose du Barry.
My shivering gelatins of surfeit faith,
factums grief
grenat bleeding, I coralline no more,
wounds sanguine,
the cruel death of color,
ponceau or rubic,
chiffonier of many drawers, creasing poultice,
to this inhabitant
in the mashes of almirah.

Mallhiola Incana, Muscari,
Ipomoea purpura, Nerine
in the herb garden of Alexander Krings,
Gloria de Dijon is welcome,
Lady's mantle sufficient among the sage.
Love in the mist keeps synergy
proviso, there between Tithonia
and the Fan flowers, oddly warmed by
ides of Galanthus, Astilbe,
Lavatera and long oaths of Snap dragons.
Truth in conveyance did not trust,
voracities of False Spirea,
so the order of British yellowheads,
felt quickened to profess.
Though conundrums of Crepe hyacinths,
fraught concern, and held inquisition as to
why Love lies bleeding, though the nettles
did not esteem, mourn nor confess.

I felt the colmar, winnower of calibre,
capstan and difficult in side scenery of breath,
an airy jocose in the curt poises of Nestor,
it was branchia or fustian, I sough to the tree.

Panting in the shrouds, as the palm leaf
of the gills, samiel the shallower of sand, condone
as ala in distentions of the rocks, respires
filiform, gusty timidities, the metal threads of chest.

Still hesitant in the emanation of Caurus,
fierce of helpmeet in the vase caves of Aeolus,
without volitiency, before the character
of Volturnus, wreath in coils, still quail the triumph
full donation, those testaments of self willed air.

Drawcansir, lighterman wind,
navicular mariner,
headland fen,
livraison gusts of the quill divers,
surrebut rejoinders
for the sail sea of oquassa,
for phial of the waves,
or jubilant plait,
liquids of other wind, propinquity,
fair lady of bluestocking,
blue of the grottoes.
Drawn to surface liters of leviathan,
fearful flagons, for those of the cloth,
pendant stories of circulating libraries,
pell of the rumbling fellows,
petitioners of the spolia optima,
redolent circumspect, in the contest for
pledging seals,
fraters neither to endorse
the gale trollers,
in Northern pride to preserve,
either diffusion of grand thunder.

She rode him gloss, the waters of chersonese,
the horse Akhal-Teke, by the name of caitiffs,
Labyrinth's lachrymation, for foal his mother lost
to the carriage car of Jagannath.

Armozeen, the fate of bullion, temporal demerit
for the cloam wept for gold, the meshing winds
of huntswoman grieving the internecine of life,
Marhra by colt of cutcherry, fell too to soke.

None the less tiling winds broke, vorticist the
evening sun, helianthin fleet, as fleece without
extincteur shone, the pentavalent star of estoile,
imprimis hearth, wherein the carotene horse glistened.

The impossible peace,
reeds of Montpellier green,
as the tarnish of azo flavin,
leaves the sapphirine skies,
trypan blue.
The last of xanthic argument,
sallow want for woad,
final leaves of chrysophenin,
emeraude and celadon,
have welcomed the Alice seed,
less the golden pheasants
of pious gamboge.
Stones wherein the field gray,
the final soldier
carried beneath the lamps
of light gunmetal,
to the sorrows of Cyprus umber,
Merida or philamot,
isamine and Veronese,
each garment heart of rose bengale,
comes to the scarlet madder.
the peach blossoms of shocking pink.

34.

Years by fear of concourse,
the boscage and the tares,
the turgid wilt,
cloth-less thigh through the briars,
the blush cut of terrors
rood alters,
lawn sleeves or mantelletta.
Chantry of the pectoral cross,
purples of Geneva bands,
rochet of the blindstory
the altarpiece of parent,
a child misspoke.
Fragile hands to the ambry,
thedralesque,
her alter stone made of flesh,
scrobis stones of breath,
the day's release
for rosary,
ecclesiastes her cathedral,
naos come cotta to surplice order.

The birdbath leaves,
fragrant spritzing of moschatel,
Adoxaceae,
thus of flowers green,
wild haste of lea.
Lacing junipers of recidivist branch,
nightjars of the Cedrus sway,
Cupressaceae,
the wrest of Thuja,
soft waverling dreams Compressa.
The shone moon on white blossoms,
Violet Caribs of torpor;
Polytminae,
Eulampus,
the extemporise love of morning.

Might I learn to speak as color,
by silent, violaceous impression,
or in moire patterns of light,
in the peaceful confetti of ophite,
in the tartans tessellate,
in irisation of Tyrian purple.
Here among the breathing number,
fellowmen of the parsec,
seeing the pinto of eyes,
Caelus there, or Via Lactea,
to quietly appraise,
the hues of night medley
or dilute dun-white.
O, to bronze diversities
of auric and the verditer
to amend philamot, to that of Goya,
heartfelt minium
to naphthylamine black,
melane for ivory,
russet wounds in crocein of skin,
to lift the tea roses,
beyond lost leagues of Javelle water.

Laccaria Ammethystina,
Amethyst deceiver,
in the coy of temperate forests,
of the lands I walk,
caress to raise, my weight on soil.
Less the distances from capitals,
pacing seed I plant,
with my wilderness compressions,
brilliant azulene,
of Entoloma hochstetteri,
or Trametes versicolor,
lacing frocks of ladies,
Phallus indusiatus.
Receiverships of earthen milt,
the spore need not offer an argument,
for in grace the foliage plant,
in finger bowls, of orange-pink,
the lying beds of
Clavaria zollingeri,
Etain violets in the midst,
there in the pedigrams, might I persist.

Sounder riposte to untwine the errors,
contra remonstrance, surrejoinder,
the feminine antiphon, the womanly oceans,
questing soluble measurements, free questions
of guess rights, feel endless the waves to rise,
ballon d'essai, emporia trials, the Are waters,
flounce to retort. Replies of kindred, beyond
the spoor ordeal or masculine frisk, cut or try,
the power of our waters, receipt to muscles,
reducing our gendered indagatives to fittings of
cork or cup. The heat of riddled denouement, of
fact finding sport, fails disinter even in rough
draft, the challenge of women, delve there the
heaven poke, of fear! Let then the down-stone
riddles resolve, we are coming for our peace,
on to the flagrant docimasy, thalassemias,
power, rebuttal! Cast all seed, it comes to nothing
beyond the soil! Look, the mighty rinse is free,
rush we must the hurry to tumult sod!

It was a wedding of two shadows,
each of the pantomimes gathered,
abiding the congregation of tones,
a fiction of leaves and a friction of ravens,
helping fable through the heavy doors.
I was there in icterous, if considering
my throne upon saffron's challis,
mikado yellow and the middle stone,
among summer's vernant guests of
aestival, to weavers hands infuscation,
I joined thus the deeper shoulders
embrown most somber. I would bring
rubor crimsoning melancholy, before
the moleskin gray of the water's reflection
made grave it's bishop's purple quivering
stria, through the iris of Monsignor windows,
as the midnight absolved, fireflies for eyebrows
in the leery visage of facsimiles quests

Light-ish to the tantalum lamp I waken,
dreams to the candlestand, leave with the
paraffin butterflies of eventide, by reeds begloom
wax.
Brise-soleil the choice of the unlit eyes open,
sashes ample the veilleuse of morning, to every
filament of lamplet willows I take, will again bedim
the clads to rest.
Here then the lumen-hours, what is Fata
Morgana, which tampers, lux the earthshine of
rutilant schemes, lampyrids of timid thought,
gesticulate.

Being as if there was a weight to the sky,
pererration, diffusion, a type of excursus
or blanch, a furtherance from the winds
of fowardal, it came without bellwether,
a gray muscularity, le pas.

I felt no transit in its shunt of step, birds
of alight did not disemplane, the flume of
rain did not debouch, waiting in the ingress,
the companionway, the adit approach, in
propylaeum, I did sense my thoughts.

Nether sun of emigre nor viaticum spoke,
will-of-the-wisps did not effuse or heather
disembogue, if there was an moment to push
the day, it would not avulse, perhaps an aside to
intermit, I by osmose returned patent, for sleep.

Near caritas, pupils of hospitality, Wisteria
Shiro-kapitan, purple raceme of confrere,
fragrant inamorata in liaisons of the weeping
willow.

Consortships of well graces, light blossoms
of soft salutations, forelocks of bowers kiss,
glad hands of fluid pergolas, tender waists
Hon-Beni.

Heigh by way the curtsies spoke, no words
of merriments fellowships told, consortiums of
anchorite, levees of maturation, convivial proximal
of insular touch.

Danae of fount, solatium, tuppence of assignat,
letter de cre'ance, the hope of palms, meed of florin.
Honorariums of the thread needle child, Schottische,
rouleau weavings of realm, gracile royalties of
courante. Hale there the Lambeth marigolds
genteel faculties of water, specie of sou, Stravinsky
fountain, wealth in consul civil, unity of sentiments
every truest wealth brought for ardor.

*Nigh-hand from the rive, or from the cleuch,
nowhere near the cotermin, your burning of
popinque or hairbreadth. Stride the foreground
of styptic pencil or cervix of emaciation, the
coarct of the belliform child, to leave by wildfire
for Ravennagrass, the cramp of ground between
us! Never the evanescence diminutive, I was the
river, to the iota of vanishing point, growing
mountains from pedigrees of monad, purlieus
vicinage of ultramundane, the wide berth of tears
for finger widths of transpacific, sand work
for the oracles of bountiful and sovereign shores.*

Where now my refuge stream, the whispers
which gave reside the tadpoles, another golden
byway in castellations of the fish, topiaries
for the battered child, filled in and buried,
a culvert made crass for yet another, awkward
carapace of human home.
Narrow the natural running ground, for those
who have fled the body traces of argument,
for the sumac, for the brown punks and every
glistening accommodation of the seed, now
dispossessed orderings, twice buried roots in
curse fleets our refuge and refuse.

I paginate to the left-hand page,
imprimatur or frontispiece,
is this flyleaf of agony columns
or feuilleton of the decoy ducks?
Brown print of letter press,
as to what thoughts are arbiter
or confidante,
what I fear of festschrift,
in hearing yenta,
Athenaeum is foundry proof,
or are the slipcases current.
In hustings I need help countrywide,
for all the bruit noise,
crier for the kern,
in folding the sways of lexicon,
for the field guides,
and the vice tomes of

Come limber leaf, transcending winds,
widening guild prolongations branches,
acceleration intumescence of honeyed sallows,
quivering though the wicking bee, may not
be worsted from autumn's crescent shadow.

Come laurel the high peaks, as the Zephyr
bear prestige, as the prominent ancillaries
fear the calumet will worsen, for rosy cheeks
of exaltation, drift faltered toward earthen
feet, ruins offering glad trays to nadir.

All Hastings of ribbons, sleepless spring
ambition, the desultory jaspe' will moire to
brighten, languishment Slough of Despond,
the Eeyorish will dance again in blithe, cordial
wind convivial, dulcet comfy gentled times.

Follow on from fountainheads, authorships
of the butterfly effect, curios of derivatives,
planetariums of a remaindered touch.
Belongings of our fingerprints, every tender
fruit of profit elucidate, delicate etymologies
of softer equilibrium. Sequel the mystic
engineering beadwork of rain, resting her
heresies hereditaments on asafoetida and
bay leaves Laura's nobilis, though wherefore
admit her search for black onions. I believe
her for I've seen her bury stones which grew
the mass bread of pimpernel.

All by roses of doyennes I weep,
for my letterhead of aiquillete,
countersigns of orchid semaphore,
each martyred veil of lambrequin,
martlet of the church bells,
the pull of faces flagging down,
the strawberry markings of fesse point.
Scottish thistle, English rose,
Welsh daffodils and the Japanese
sun rising, markings to be felt while
sejant, letterings of aftermath,
paraph or stigma.
Dimidiates of impress foreign affections
of sigil, or as shibboleth,
the odd weeds of Turkish crescent,
and the watchword of oriflamme,
here Gillette's differencing,
affections less to hyphenate,
wreath or bays the brassards detect.

She had brought plainchants, songs Gruss An
Aachen, flowers by the bow, col arco, Gruss An
Teplitz, hymns to my sleeves, by grace note, pauses
of retenu did not hold back, in musica ficta, nor
feeling fauxbourdon, Athene figures phrasing.

She was the white rose, The Poet's wife, I
the Alnwick rose, in the soft postern of Tangles
and Tatjana, I could not discern either pavane nor
e'tude, past my quotients to listen, after Friesia.

I was caught by her in Sparrieshoop, in slips
of pale pink, Souv. De Mme. Leonie Viennot,
her beauty would not be assembled in asserts of one
name, not by sixth or diminished sevenths, passions
signatures, Claire Matin, Clea's rose, garden
contents she would settle, long before the snows.

The faint phrases, the crying down,
animadversion, flays of squib,
pasquinade, twirling child,
will you find lambs redound the spit?
Article to the taste of black raspberries,
nectar opposing the skinning of the tongue,
write for the braided fires,
inveigle the okra flowers, bonnet heavy
the fragrant towers!
Meet elder your ovations,
your meed for the unrevered,
the gardens lionize felicities,
watch commend, as every blossom,
doffs their hats.
Winds condone their gyre beside you,
abrading memory, they brought their lyrics,
to the sorrows of transgression,
sing encomium, imprimaturs of mint,
costmary, lovage,
comfrey, marjoram, capsicum and mace,
live sanguine the hallowed!

To mishandle of censor, or in lithe of pardons,
neither by appanage, her beauty, she took light rein,
my hands beneath Sarvis holly.
Her kiss of admiral, arboreal her pardons permit
winged fruits, what she earthed of Huisache or
softened abdications of Japanese Zelkova.
She did not relinquish, her mercies from Sephora,
supine her cessions of flowers, she abject certain citadels
paladins of the butterflies, her ravelin prevail.

Come passage forward, seedlings of metamorphosis,
without abridgments the days of change,
braised of fruits faisan appetites.

Light is growing the rounded crowns of the Winged
Elms, and Threeflower Hawthorns, beside
the ornamental edges of the waters.

The rivers run sweet for the Tag Alders, Alnus
rugosa, (Du Roi) Spreng, veinlets of full rows,
dull dark green the sap ladders beneath.

(Ait.) Willd, Hazel sisters, winter will shelter, male
catkins and feminine cones, aromatic the years to come,
leaf futures brightened in 3-angled pith.

Bereaved earth viduous,
grass widow,
if lost the jointuress whence,
eons lief her long service,
her womb without red,
Eden flowers disposed by industry,
blues begone the bee.
Perennial memories,
wreaths in rape of dry constants,
arables of willows fotting
an Ethiopian skin,
all set squares in the plazas of oaks,
felled wounds of timeless pillars.
She fed the thieves,
offering yields to the stolid,
the dead remain at her bosom,
for the chosen resurgence of the goad,
mourners weeping thought her tampion,
never cognizant she bright tyler,
is the Christ.

A drowsy rain with misgivings, tapering on worn
grasses of raillery, remit hearing serpentines
of melodies, persiflage of chaff.

Weeping the lots of Calcutta sweep, an umbilical
hour in fortuities of sun, clotures of mist which
did not come, light impulses of Coelebs stager.

The fountainheads of purview, reck spinster roots,
detenu in vigil of gifts, found the mount guard
needy, tun, prudent promises reconnoitered.

It is Wednesday of the rising wheelwright,
the whisper spoken has drained the bells,
Black Kniolas festal, bayhops amain for haste,
prochien ami actuary, conservators of light.

The marcescence, the withering, confound
to transfigure, conversions of betterments,
wine presses in the caste marks of sun, cider makers
weaving, for panting dances of fitter's chance.

It is full house for the flint maker, trim by
heart the cures of dawn, brief turn the yards of
flowers, fitness in preparator color, well suited
requisites of verdant verdigris and violets.

I live the realms of teacups,
posey's of wegotism settle on the shelves,
beetlings of the lap-streak,
in rodomont of flora paintings,
a pound of words for the proprietorship.

A fine gram of sugar, whereby,
the coxcomb lay, in transilience of violets,
assuage to sheaths of calumet,
ornature of Morisco, or lister of acanthus,
warming atlantes, in billet of caryatides.

All cloisonné in repoussage of
illustrious women, less champleve' chip,
falters to the rotations of public tranquility,
to meniscus tears in Huygenian of Campani's
eyepiece, the frock of beauty left.

By word of the companionable, it was a proscenium
fire, in sparing of amadou and chestnuts,
but I thought irascible, as did the link-men of the
avenues, a thrift not in the fellowship of facts.

The fusee and the tandsticker were northernmost
kindle, the present sorority of the aurora which
likely gave umbra to the ardency of shadows, this
trifling of caper or Cossack of flambeau.

Frater, frater or firebrand of equal fill, tinder
ceorl those denizens which unbridled manumit flames
that night, for every anatripsis of novel despite, felled
more of Marrowfat peas than peatland turf might.

Keeping pleat the strewn pace of aventurine,
upon the pahoehoe and bronze of tall grass,
they give their ingots as gifts to my path, sterling
too for the shadows, my alloy of cupronickel.

Arapahoe by way of subtleties, illustrators
scribing Arbutus in dew, sullen pauses when
incline isn't true, traversing linear joys, glad
gatherings of earthshine ascensions golden noon.

There will be the shale and the stone face to
come, hardness of the bramble and the way-bridge
of the thorn, though the weavers take the sweater
home, Geist enshrines the view.

Scripp's Murrelet, sestina, sensum
terpsichorean silhouette,
semanteme shriver to surmount,
skies Sedalia and the sea of throng.
Imaginations of feathers,
the two voices of equivoque,
weaving wings through quester
searching for the fish of piscator.
Curia of lapis, Areopagus of blue,
and the reflexes of antistrophe,
in the quotients of chant,
Shrike for the followers
of semaphore and the riposte
signaling.

Penstemon Blackbird, Penstemon Strictus
somewhere mute below the opal clouds,
thick refractions of dark purple among the
inscrutable opacities, lour the scrim of vanities
from windowpane.

Penstemon angustifolius, the stains of Alice
Hindley, Andenken an Friedrich Hahn,
in subtractive hues of gouache, soft indistricts
of tenebrous, of gossamers in the storm shroud
laces of showcase.

Penstemon digitalis, Cobaea beardtongue,
there be miasmic in the praises spoken, tertiaries
of subtractive color; floss in the voile, a film of
nightshade mourning enhanced, scarlet bedim
the burst bruising etiolates.

Crotchetier enchant pinioned Stevedores,
lettering feathers of speaking tree,
whistlers and pin wheels of sentiment,
the rhymes of wayward or fleet.

Grane for Sigurd, shire horse of mystics,
or Odin less consistent, Sleipnir by
gaits tongue twisted, dare number the
pass of fools who trotter believe.

The common truths of sumpter mule,
Shetland, Black Saladin or White
Surrey, circumspect the greater elegance
than the steed of Rustam, lame portent.

Capricious chariots, the notional chantress
by the commanders of the Kittiwakes,
chaperon the billet deux of cautions tender,
in push pin trees, of yews devout.

Tender marginal, manna of skin, soft précis,
Qistibi, the bread of habitations, Obi Non
supplicant touch of flour, yeast and milk.

Rose water curtesies in solartium as soigné,
leaven of Zopf, widows plait for brioche
in flaccid requiem of husbands felling.

Rising memories, figures of press and tactile
silence, sharing Injera, Naan of hearth, divine
affinities of warming bread, fleshes of Vanocka.

Waifs of grain drift forward towards maturity,
elders of summer, summations of fall,
on breeze of devoirs, good wishes,
sweet kindred, let us meet again in May.

Waiting again for the cattails to reach my height,
beside the steams as waters unction,
my year for you, is a generation,
yet I jubilant in your embodied presence.

Currant Clearwings work cocoons of wool fell
weaving through the Wisteria vines cradles
belaying christening introductions, debutant
purples in silken flights, parvenu or roturier.

It was the bell shaped hour when I found the
pear; before I came to the turning acriform of
maple leaf, with its conduits and its seams, its
ruche edges by the short leads of shirr.

Among the inlets, and thrice the vale, beyond
the crenate of the incisural trees, to pleasures
orchids, by lapel and Vandyke collar, to pectorals
and cupola that brought hillock to the face.

There plicate by collapse of day, the neaten seed
in annular of the sunflowers, from such ample
coronet, I have not left even-side, nor walked gonion,
from the spoken axis of chiasmus poets.

A submission of gray found harm in the glebe,
her small resignations of palm, her gown also
was a cast of shade, I dressed in charlatanry
that day, between the grape house and the bone
dust, Sumar May near Mallory.

Far too young for consanguinity, too tender
the cherish, her horizontal rose of lamentation.
Below a mount of sky, I washed her in Stygian
creek, calm before her own Rhadamanthus, I
bare not usher what harbinger had taken.

Sweet paynim her love for James, she kept no
other arm as Shepard, hidebound her mortal wince.
A hereabouts of flowers I lay at her breast, offering
the apocryphal lace to dissidence hands, gladful
withered there, her edicts black spire.

The cuttings speak, glossolalia of flowers,
sighs before the chant, proems of terrarium,
the cuttings speak in pithily, citing flutes beguile,
Adam's apple.

Though lesser the soft palates of vocal forms,
farewell encomium, averment the strine of leaf,
common they weep their civilizations, contractions
in diminutions of chorus.

Parlance of the Matriarchs, English greed,
might the fortunes of chrestomathy find mankind
short of breath, haste succinct those fools who
prune the air, truncate!

Tracing her cadence by Sandaled anemones,
her sandy slips of white sea cucumber, in the
gait of two rivers, was Solimoes loving, her
water's foals running the shores of Portuguese
Encontro das Aguas, past all soldiers in grief
of her prize.

The burning of ribbons, the cession of leaves,
through and past her scholar, will the roses
graduate, Belle Portugaise, but her first
pursuant brought her a nation of lavender, in
him the grief strings of fado.

It was not known if there be a wedding of
swallows, or figurines given Alcochete, as
Beatriz devoted her joy to the receptions of
Balearic shearwaters, principal finery of the
Dunlins, beauty gathered none away.

Stealing chessman from the walrus's,
assuaging mythos by the unicorn throne,
false descriptors of flesh and bone,
by lives of profit, not your own.

Once by birds, boasts of feathered hats,
passerines in velvets of millinery cast,
summer songs of tendering flights,
in petulant displays of insular glass.

Fallen quick for flourish foods the Fennec
fox, err of forages foment our feasts,
all fattened contrarians afore the beasts,
sharing none of courage, as Ruppell's fox
deceased.

All the Falco are born to spring, every Merlin,
or Common Kestrel, Gyrfalcons as well as
Claravis and Laughing doves, beside the hard
seeds coming, Sugar Ann peas and Cloudberries.

What grows from May of Ashmead's Kernel,
of Frequin Rouge or Dabinetts, Elderberries of
long vine, holding notions of Aleutian time, of dials
Chamorro, and as well lands of Myretoun Ruby.

Lulworth butterflies revisit the long past of Erica
Darleyensis. Blues to Daboecis, the Commas and
the Checkered white, Mourning cloaks in the pearls
of Cosmos, reed for reed, sugars of Bouvardia.

Trompe l'oeil, sfumato
the nude or aerial perspective,
contemplating the found object,
limn or cross hatch of thought,
the chasing of the cameo.

With solvents or by turpentine,
the bone carving of the shadows,
scene paintings, sand castings,
cire perdue, the kinetic bronze
rivers of annunciation.

An oud wind speaking to the
aquarellists, fete galante, the
conversation piece, atelier, camera
lucida versus the museum's retable,
finding home penorcon unstable.

The beginning walk was a moil,
a fetch in the reflex of St. Mary's thistle,
a reentrance of the helix,
before coming to the aisle of grass,
dandelions of loggia,
a covered way, Fabian of the woods,
of the golden tortoise,
with wild violets in the furls.
Spring was in its honeymoon period,
breezes in homecoming,
following the fragrances of watershed,
every conjure in remake of flowers,
each leaven to and fro in protean
of metamorphosis.
By the time the day fell quorum,
labile I lay where the clouds undressed,
ephemeral, oscillating, ill beset the dressmaker,
whose threading forbad mercurials,
soft, fluctuating emendations,
the alchemist nature,
drafts of cogent reformations endearing,
a charitable, benevolent skin.

Characters cochineal, Serin finch or Schalow's
Turaco, asmine feathers with Loden green leaves on
oval peripheries, crowns of hanging flowers fuscous,
dun, Demerara , imperial purple spinnerets.

Avid pink of Coquerel's Coua, Luma white braille,
fuchsia rings of fleur de lea, beneath water silk eyes
of lapis lazuli, amaranth of tufted Coquettes, follow
rosaniline, Bali Bird of paradise, flights of Kagu's.

Naive jade of Chinese drawing letters, are written
press, retort designations impressed in feathers of
Impeyan Monal and Swinhoe's Pheasant, xanthene
bands, canscent silver, pomelo or gentian prose.

Budgerigar's, Ibis and Temminck's Tragopans,
carry cerulean, musical symbols upon their chests
cinnabar affectations of orange pekoe and massicot
in spring or sallow regions, songs roan or niello.

The headwind took a musical first chair,
feckless, tacit hands, deft fingers,
a paragon stringer which brought it's instinct,
Perth operetta, to the sonnet trees.
If wizardry were felt, inhale and exhale,
a proficient polymath, or gifted
mystagogue, handedness was breathing,
in harness as the madrone bent.
In Renaissance of my impressions, perhaps
the Siskiyou mountains were pushing
back, but seneschal had not practiced the sage
of Rasputin, as had the custodial trees.
As was as if, the gales of magnum opus had
not encountered the cultivars of the Elfins,
in the care of husbandry, I kept possession,
my rein of scarf, as aft Bows Fedora!

They had coupled by clothing, or this was my first
swath of mantle thinking, the two of them in
conferences of indecision, Mao jacket or redingote,
exacerbations ending in paletot.
She in gored skirt pruning Norton's attentions,
not that philibeg again darling, wear the backless,
the chapeau's at Le Madeleine bring mass to sighs
at the transoms of that winding sheath!
I was very much in picture hat, until he fled door
without her, I should be home by two Essa, don't forget,
ring your mother, she's in widow's weeds again,
and make sure Raymond is out of here, I despise
his himation and his wool coat.
Matrimony in pinstripes was my Capris in short
legged confusions, nuptials of the three piece suit, but
was wig beard actually, Raymond in her lisle stockings,
and Balmoral was heavy on my gallon hat,
I excused myself taking deerstalker out the door!

For Ciba, light blue captions,
livid blue announcing skies,
for Ciba, who atones in soft plebiscites
Lammas Day, Scilla siberica.

For Ciba, gifts of brass rubbings,
weatherings phthalocyanine,
brindles of indigo, her Blue Niles crying
perturbations of Strawberry mark.

For Ciba, skimming bluets, Sedge sprites,
how softly she adapts the damselflies
humming, her heavens songs of Robin's egg
blue, heart's stria shells, yokes breaking.

The changing voice of thunder, tones through Ikshu, clement the Zikak cane, the requital of tu quoque, auditoria's above the munificence of sugarcane.

It be again the voice of Ivan, forever flee the rudder of quail, cacophonies like the boisterous voices of shouting males, where the gentle cider of golden rods weeps.

N in guides of winter North, ample grapple the pitch, atmospheric the oars of Thor, waters yet tremble, if light presents, rise then unsettled waters, to another cycle of portend prince.

Freshet, braiding bourne, confluent stream,
silt of the river Darling, redress the sedentary
dreams in rushes forward, for Waratah, for
Telopea.

Cast down my efforts to the root, I crown
the concourse with flowers, holding no purpose
for the seabeds, I persuade Geraldton wax,
And Violas.

Fertile below Umbilicaria, fond of Benth hills,
Banksia, Swainsona, wealth green fields just
beyond the swales, glen occasions rains peculiar,
Ash Quandong, Acacia elata.

A mural of Peltogyne,
painters of unripened reseda,
natives of amaranth,
reticulations of plaster,
brought a beautiful fidelity
to the nescience woods of Purple Heart.
Numeracies in gnosis of leaves,
sophistries of the unlettered artist,
lines in foresight of acuity, remaindered
time, in delicate, warm distortions,
misnomers of textures,
tender discordances of highlights,
tyro days, of expatriate elders.
Cognizance in due passage,
I felt the air of wallows,
in light headed passage,
donnish templates of the peace,
that principal hour of old hand,
pausing extricably the rote,
a date of wrinkled fingers,
passing tenderest visage,
simpler qualities across my face.

Counsel free choir Emily, mornings glories
have opened, and your glove puppet is making
kite strings, tether glee fight!

Soft of Eye splices and Prusik knots, Emily,
form the Rigid-Heddle looms, from Inkle, I
will unbraid your hair or burden thought.

From the cordgrass and spiked Ravenna,
Emily, your chrysalis in Purple millet, in dine days
I find you, early violets without aspic.

To warming May, your child stone Emily,
tears dissipate quickly, quiet seed in Adam's apples
of carry Crows, as Kaiser-i-Hind purpose there.

I looked through her eyes of lonely buildings,
entrances of Sorghum trees through the broken glass,
torn wallpaper Petrouchka Flock, wrinkled birdsongs
fluttering from the tears of Faversham Moss.
Murmuring due, the broken forays, a velvet pattern
christened Brer Rabbit, wainscoting bleeding
the blood rain of years, a frail tone which blanched from
heart, less pallid assertions present in her dress of ivory.
From scaffolds contrite of fallen shelves, expenditures
Elizabethan, where in amber her pace, the Sycamore's
grew sullen, pessimism in her threads of brambles,
buttons of Oakum hooks, in bare redress her collar bones
did forge ample, posterns of frail chest.

Breeding consciousness
among us, cultivars and comets,
the awareness of flax,
writings of the Mangroves,
the receding joy of dolphins
galas of dorsal fin.
Houses of the weaver bird,
architects of Madonna,
loss of turgor in touching stimulus,
leaving waters of Mimosa Pudica,
the ancient fingers prints of Sequoias.
Sentimentality of Keta Salmon,
for their birthplace,
the migrations of latitudes,
by Sternidae and Red Phalaropes,
dances of Parotia,
aviators of the Violetears,
endless gallantries of visceral procreation.

Buoyant reseda, color of hope,
Orange flower oil,
Persian violets, Exacum affine,
the spirit term of tone, rest this
suffice mask behind capercaillie,
variegates shift schist of stone.
The chersonese isthmus,
in lamella of browns,
or terrane of pink carnations,
feeling more of blue coryphaeus,
as catechumen skies fellow violet,
and orients of sable anneal,
adieu the niello night.
Coppering skin of condisciples,
gules of humming, green cicadas,
Morgan side of emerald beetles,
hatchling birds sallowed,
from mothers sought discrownment,
golden leaves of latent June,
aubergine appeals of Indigo buntings,
dappling chests in imperial misrule,
ripened boysenberries.

Granting peace to the barbarians, holly prizes to
the fists of crease, giving assets accede to mutilators,
we attest will illume, grisly thoughts to growing
flowers <.

The Orcus who bring Gatling to feminine parts,
volley breast in orbitals of crucial wrecking balls,
conceding operable cloud lands in compliant
equitations upon request <.

Ophiolaters of the peace, trust upon ophidian
snakes, branching ingots, making philosophical
terms opera seria, for last anguish of young
woman, their screaming registers unheard <.

Foolish schisms liaise the beasts, fragments
of a gender, conjoin extirpated upon the spits of
peace! Shadoof and Persian wheel, this hour,
to the supercilious leaders of three nations <.

On pillows of rising water, armor flanks of sleep
foster at littoral edge, sidestroke in crowds of weather,
poison tributaries, such blemishes from the flocks of
stone.
I oil baleful, something dark in the lamp, told to
follow indices of the branches, though of the hundred,
each bent in its own error, cilia leaves of red
nictation.
Amblyopia visions the eyes at depth, forms of hydros,
Aube through the cotton, seiche the nightmare in spate,
off soundings of Charybdis and Amphitrite, the floating
wolves have spoken.
The bollard child, profiles of Gokstad slowly excavating,
elder sea-shawl the land digests. The Blueman fjords
of the bald-pated moon, where the garboard strake, ON
meginhufr flounder.
Thoughts of peck or pica, in Gunter chains of boundless
feathers, find temper's long hundred weight, coifs of comb's
order, left column's inch debarking, rust of the tree nails,
mire sluice purling sault, quilts of the seasick, fluviomarine.

Argali, O. Ammon,
lambs,
Mouflon, O. Aries,
O. Nivicola, Snow sheep,
ewes baring soft Cheviot,
Kerry Cade call pasture,
Galway sheep,
Valais blackface,
to Briza media,
of round leaved sundew.
Purpose the Shepards,
insular for the wool,
Donegal tweeds convertible ,
Brome, barren,
Brome, soft,
Marram grass,
Argali, O. Ammon,
Mouflon, O. Aries,
inquiring O. Nivicola,
shawl of winters sweet.

The earth grows inside us,
the cognizant child as the new rains
endow scent, or relish the reeds
in riches of more luminous color;
variable clouds of motion,
alterations in speed of rain.
We all have our own tree rings
wide and narrow years,
not yet earth at rosebay,
nor tamarisk, nor symplocus,
little quaking grass, nor burdock,
though through her boneset,
Viola would keep testament,
her courses of creeping buttercups.
Sweet ringed children of the snow wreaths,
denouements yarrow, the cognizant year
of nandin, nandina,
fruit bearing, profiting.

Arbres Remarquables, on that day of cognizance,
a child awakened by the earth, Allouville-Bellefosse,
the contiguous priest made it's chapels of initial heart,
Chamber de L'Ermite, Notre Dame de la Paix.

Nandin, Nandina, fields at rosebay, burdock though
through her bonesets, sweet ringed children of winter
wreath, tamarisk and symplocos, profiting fragrances
of early Violas, Chateau de Vaux-le-Vicomte.

I who wed young Mayenne, came to tears Jouanne,
though I wash near Bernay, in Charentonne, in sovereign
cleanse of three rivers, drier the shielding towels of aiding
sun, straightway the flesh, I have loved no other.

Thin materials,
membrane and lining paper,
lamelliform in propinquity,
soft purlieus of finger breadths,
yet the grazes at elbow
are lonely.
Of coterminous,
and the rubbing kiss,
the caesura and the horizon,
the scissure and the shelf of
intermission, the substratum
of neighboring coats,
trepan the riddles of teabags
and colander.
Candor pull open
sincerities, the plain words
of birth, leaving cribrous
the nave, mornings
left ajar, for beyond bodkin,
there is the space between orgasm
and heart.

Caught by swimmer's habit, her bower mood
of doubt, a fate of nomadic itinerary, on the calves
of eyot, turtle shell in hand, postulating jounce
jewels in her suspicions of malfeasance.

There I stood solid on her atoll, jellify in sight
of hadj, in her paper eyes of tidal moods, a mutable
lukewarm volatile dissolving, tasked by the clink
of assignation, petite addressing circumscribea.

Who are you and why do I find your crowd in
unbound prurigo upon my stretch? Are you island
mother of this sea girt, prejudice me I ask, might
I flow out, though hoping to bring coquet to rest!

I swim here combine daily, by toss and task,
resolute my years without the accent of such pulse!
I amend my heart grew louder at your approaching
caprice, kittlish she was to praise feathers tickling.

Tea's - Darjeeling Margaret's Hope,
Yin Zhenceleste,
darling Karas Choat,
caressing certain pressures of fingertips,
delights to elicit,
dampened sighs from porcelain.
A morsel dropped, of Pu-erh,
raising pitch, in premise of leaf,
both vegetal and vanilla notes,
and perhaps dark dragons,
in delightful delicacies
of floral temperament.
There is a stone with a ring bore,
aligning center table,
her morning portion fresh by air,
of Kiptagich Purple oolong,
offering mineral and artichoke notes,
tomorrow dark liquor
in tomes of leather and undergrowth,
Kukicha Stemgreen,
her way of finding earth,
per tear, craft swelters atone.

The interruption, Cistothorus and the musician wren,
ruined tranquility and the audible contraptions,
a sovereign to the marriage of peace and candlelight,
the stillness of a woman finished by boisterous men.

Apolinar's and Flutist wrens, Nava's to the serenity
of breast, beside the silent feathers, cacophonies of
the metropolitan chest, the sanguine and the high note
of harmoniums, the beating of ambulatory avenues.

Willows of Scarlet curls, whispering to their wind lovers,
I may intrude such felicitations to collect, eavesdrop of
Portmanteau, pleasance frail, commotion will fail sighs,
on the fitful mornings, patron pratfalls neglect.

Come to Amur Maackia, come cornucopia,
bracing shoulders of staves decoctum,
limber tempering bound-ish hearts Aotearoa,
Anne Marie Trechslin.

In reeds of rain, on fell bales harvesting, the
drinking of Johnathon's, blushes soaking
Gala, yellow xanthins Idared, artesian's cast in
fluid fain of autumnal muscle, passions
met of season.

Bordure Nacree, Clair Matin her archway of
six roses, supplicant breezes her sighs in
Vive, thrive again forward springs, Clea's Roses,
Belle Poitevine awaiting her gaining sounds,
of filling leaves come entry.

*Most of life we didn't build, as we function in
preexisting structures, the old growth and the
autobahn, transits of cypress for aggregate stone.
Hundreds fore our trace of land, ampules of this
earth, agile beauty the fragments we walk, my
lover true. This garrison window others will
use, on the hour my flesh is done, I will sleep
in you, this closed heart of worship, not knowing
the long spines of Juniper which surround me.
Perishables here I suffer, forgetful relinquishments
of the boundless views wherein my thoughts
your graces planted, a parcel of all returnees,
to the chilling order of this womb, recount me in
my dying the tiny wakes of grass, being feathers,
the streams of drinking hares, I postpone before
such harvests, how devout this wrestling heart
pleasured docile sprigs, darlings of arduous habitat,
bitter forbade I can't take with me, gracious daily,
neither portrait or friend.*

The sun turned left onto Meredith, moving remunerations
to the frugal horns of cicada's song, with warming shoulders
I step in balance, the regal rays of dawn, paradigms fortuitous
peaceful ascent.

Breezes of oklava fold upon the Rymin rye, lifting lightly
slight debranned grains in it's whist of baskets, briefs of
quiet force engaging my paces, wherein delights it's excitations
scurry.

I to the sorting rare pleasures, found Criollo beside the
the Dutchman's pipe, leaves of Huichol parting the awakened
mists, calm my own wavering breath, farriers present moistened
with glee.

Of curving inwards the cove could not raise itself
from the kerf, fosse among the heights, a plicature
depression at the pectorals of mountains, a laugh line
beside the sea.

Sands syncline, flutings to the will of water, from blue
wreath it could not disentangle, linear quarrels flattened
in course of writhe orbicularties, ambit, rotary, contrarians
undeviating.

Portend the honorables if wisdom proffer, Cumberland's
of Olive Ridley, halos of Chelonia mydas, beading egg
within these sands of round skirt, meniscal mendicant
truth pert shall boast.

Nutrients this caress Hoya Kerrii,
reaching summit queries in heart customs
Katsura, the fells then of rain,
the hand gatherings of eclecticism's,
damp, idiosyncratic beads for rosary.
Deviations subtle heels, Lithops
gardening nearest passions
privatized as living stones,
firm belongings beyond
rigorous intolerance,
such plebiscites of ground.
The naked men among the Orchids,
never clothe, but here tergiversates,
Janus neither variegations,
flights of tabulations
of white egret flowers,
nor bias the oracles of sighs,
in distant ascensions,
the accruement shift,
elegance of bearing stem or neck,
these leaf hearts Eucalyptus.

The foliage of ice, jittering waters,
the anxiousness of lakes,
their friendship mists remembered,
joy for their rains rejoinder,
the centenarian clouds of thousandth estuaries,
the heart lock of silver ferns,
banns for carry
the January rivers defend against
a De-palming sun.
Full bodies of mere,
the counts from rillets heat will take,
late June battlements with Aquarius,
as she sheld her artesian,
in shyest similes where cygnets
by comfort contained her,
wishes deport of fiery plans,
her capful of sea,
gratuitous of feather
and of stone,
for vessel her legend children
in shelter conscious to marry,
selves without convection rebound.

I hear you observing, a tilt in the voice,
from satire to inclement,
a more random ornament,
tincture's iridescent in the particles
of hue.
Thermal stress, or amorphous solid,
auroral glass,
Ididill as the sun unbroken,
retentive light which retains it's order,
engrams conserving,
unlike obtuse pieces.
Incubus to revenant,
love cannot abide the unfounded
numerals,
or visionaries recompense,
the eye may see but singularities,
populous lady of kaleidoscope,
will not be found or find,
ither solid,
love or home.

Tilings perhaps of plein-airist or poetic kineticist,
hardened incising postconcretist,
copperplate tinting clay words, statuaries
of mono winds with scenewright meanings.
Gilded idealist of rye vignettes, processes bound
in dry points of zincograph, should the light
feel better than tan or Paul Ricault be conferred
with greater burin purple. There is that drawer
of water just beyond where the sand knobs
begin, pulling from the active world, lure
yet, waves again, but the aquarists and
marine painters must model the consenting impress,
dreams depicting slenderest focus. Eakins, Delacroix
and Ozenfant caravan to move the view, as does
the aquarist writer mouldering words unist, such
temperaments preserving poptical artists.

More sanitarium than blue, the agregis sky,
plenaries of storm, thunder's propulsive hearsay,
archeries of lightening, salvo's of asylum,
occidental hail, skeet, detonations, wild shivering
of pipetting walls.
Graft of dun, less coalescent light, this blindfold
worn is the tissue of the clouds, rancors banding
the angry eyes, gray obtuse, chilled, tumultuous
gyre, mercies disgraceful harassing stones, light
apprised to granite.

Nierembergia surrounding, she married,
Tophet, in deference to minuets,
in avaricious alter, by will of caitiff,
her minuend to entrammel.
Obedience full consortium,
she became reach greetings of his hand,
her beauty blackening,
full will with remission,
she was her husband and therefore a man.
Pejorative cleaning the eunuch flute,
her quantifying onion of weeping ends,
gravamen song contumelious singing,
she the 6th digit in the rind of his hand.
His jonquils expanding as she absolves,
paragon flowers of parsimony,
having married charities of self missives,
benefits magnanimous, unwittingly
selfishness finds him kissing only,
his own empirical ends!

Jurisconsult, barren peach tree, assumpsit of December's
discrowned sun, pugnacious disputations of fruitless attendances
in mora of wastrel's branch, thrive in replevin the extravagant
demand, orchards to terrace, a huis clos, oblique natural orders,
prorogues per demand.

Flordacrest or Carored, by yellow dances Fond du Lac,
come the tympan or the lamella leaf, in the petal of full season,
there will be licit flowers in ridicule of reason ere the darkness
adjourn, premise thrive thereby the light, surrebutter serve writ,
sighting grace of bitter season.

Bohn the illustrations of light, bright birds
of morning mezzanine, periodic oratress among
the kittiwakes, pittites of flowers, breezes of Eng.
theatre, golden tortoises intramural light's
ambition.

Might I here, a copper intermission?

Lowering candles to the sequins of horizon ,
breast of evening, intercession as flames dismast,
wreaths refulgent lain to ground, requiescat in pace,
the shadows leave in silent chiaroscuro,
ci-git.

Might I here, oil of floating lanterns?

The hour transposes, trespasses of Somerset,
foresight of mature season, clarets resurgent
compline to chersonese, morning's ruby whisperings
of Myrana, patois of Lepistemon, Mary of olives,
new labor.

Hand giving transfers, comely chirography,
passage fasteners of heart, trysting places of
retinues, mousseux, intumescent leaflets proposing,
ornaments sequela in soft remittance, heirlooms
of hemming shadows.

Letters of shoal press supine, the glyphs of
figurina, merits of paper where hearts of intaglios
rest upon her pillows, notan daughters black
and white.

Pleasantries leaning in draughts of tablature,
pentalpha principles of her stars, mullets five by honor,
leafing skies of symmetrical beauty, all be it to limn
of poetry, marmorean touches values Parian,
quint passions of pentad hearts.

Always petting the candle light,
briar wick of paraffin
uviol lamps by oil's incite,
chartreuse,
the braise of stars.
Owlet's walking the gables of Aries,
leaving lashes to the flame,
slender calefactions, duelists replevin,
fire eaters, fair to grief.
Late August of mulberry,
certain within sires of peat,
conceive the lads of noon less creative,
than cinder nights mosaic sate,
hire heft,
the stronger pectoral spark.
Leavening sulfurs, merrymaking,
for daughters without, the lights of sheath,
more piquant blush sustaining,
saffron moments, trembling white
ingots of crimson mantelpiece.

Glass art marbles…
satellites wet mint purple,
Christiansen agates,
Veiliglass wire pulls, Seahorse orange,
blue tang, play of childish planets.
Vaseline glass,
helmet clays or watermelons,
hand-mare orbits of morning glories,
Jabo, Peltier,
buddings of interior breath,
inside the rainbows,
successor's games of 4 veined cat's eyes,
per Akro, Das purple,
Ghost marbles of brushed conquerors,
translucent redwoods, ravenswood black,
green glass of enchanted forests,
Cairo Heaton,
lavender fluorescents, re-agent plums,
aquatic brown or ruby dragons,
King Vacor dreaming,
nightshade comets,
Cadmium stars or light bound clearies.

Sulids song from the Floratam,
Sanderlings serenades from the sea grass,
from the reed splines, tomes of splendid reminiscers
gamelan orchestras of Pomarine jaegers.

Custos breve in half rest of clouds, ottava
wings of passage, Ash split songs of cane or
chantress, soft diesis of Akepa, tercet orange mediant
melodies, Dorian blues of presa hosts.

Bouteloua or lovegrasses, Coix lacryma-jobi,
Oriels of Oryza humming, leitmotivs of soft strains,
inland winds among the Teff, patina songs of lemongrass,
yellow Sordo of sweet Saccharum.

Volatile interior exclamations silent under mute
warning, the voice broken in the skirmish, this
mountain would fall in silence, and comets came
though the earth neither groan, as the water free
flower wilts on mornings unannounced.
Tears which looked toward Paijanne, derivations
the stones absorbed, Ladoga cups or furlongs far
from Mille Lacs, the rogueries of savage, weeping
salts villanelle, though welcome blood be spilled,
the scoffers of crossings, the pitted child fills.
By the long hour of mercenary, the sight of unerring
ravens, I took callow; suspicions of color; profligacies
of red, the cavities of gray, ointment and the misplaced
eye, thief vitiate the unsafe prelapsarian of pupils, the
guileless given brow to black.
The conscionable adults holding to principal voice,
the hex of silence has many, all malediction judge the
fool, but the tike of hellfire plenty, and the arch friends
by sounds of nether world, should there the judges perspire,
though the small one be found a choir singing!

Too much noise in the silence.
notations of love for the onion skins,
the heart in making.
bows of mesrichord,
long handed K in sealing wax,
born the night of Cupid's injured hand,
priors before the rose.
Priors before the rose,
first insteps of longing, the unrest of hope,
desire bring the leader of the flesh,
downfall trellises of Daughter's gifts,
attires of serendipity,
qualities of Flemish lace
requires of breast, paintings of Santvoort,
soft captives sold of Regentesses,
Matrons of the braid.

I walk the weatherboards and up the tent, applying
the revetment of arras and fascia, weeping macadam
the bed clothes for the peruke of thatch, sheath by hooded
gauze the modest veneer of hatless soils.

Homo-erectus, homocentricity, the crux depths of bus
station thinking, missing tegmen, testa and seed coat,
for the coverlets and the armor of may all, find beauty
thinning, lap robes of missing pampas.

Interiors of broadloom carpets, meadows of Portland
cement, much in fleece of exoskeletons, or counterpanes
of chitin, the eyes of equidistance by the scute of tears,
concedes canopies to ciborium indifferences.

Comforting Batiste, placing soft wrap around
yesterdays's shoulders, cajoling the wandering horizons,
tears of unknown edge, past Courbet's marine, leaflet
memories pressed under sextants of soil and grass,
adrift calendars of casual meandering.

Recesses speaking for the pre-chant skies of saints,
past braille lace flowers, unstitches of memories, absentee
segments of Chantilly, linear definitions in courses of objects,
should the base knots of beginning threads, be covenant to
me, every tailor, a bidden bind coming?

To frighten the thicket it's impasse, sickle in sprites
of endless dispatch, some be the path of weeds, an excess of
exercise, keeping callous the palms of days, search the felling
for a way, cutting the scaffolds of knuckles, skin of slivers,
dreads grains in obliques of hardwoods.

Isleteer of floating shore, desiring orientations
of Samothrace, solitaire some land back of Sulcata
tortoise, light lines in the dark case of shade.
Recalibrations of objects I saw elongated within
the sea spray, wet aspects in pinch of globes.

The moon in it's Deja Vu, perpetuities returning,
dreamful water's of Contessa, courtship to her rising,
though the moon never shall touch, her languid ebb
rescinding, nor maya disassemble dowsinger's wish,
creasing tide, as poorest conduct of linen.

Hierophant of phases, full or crescent, weeping thrice
the impervious eye in totemistic eons of blackness,
unction without chasuble or tallith it's character unseen,
toggles yet as suffragan, memory movements of mistress,
when the sea of tranquility, lay still beside her.

Mirth of Kelgia Anne, poseur, pride of Campani's
eyepiece, hand mirror of the waters, Huygenian of
shadow; Doric upon the galeiforms of stone reflecting,
beautiful boasts of apical heavens.

Impieties of Gerrie Hoek, or tartuffish Florence
something of twice raffia in the braille winnowing of
the felled Ashe, perspicacities in of the boughs, recherché
in negative oculus in dégagé light.

Then the Banian days of dearth clouds, as sylph
of rain departed, found buncombe purling, Dahlia
coccinea keeping shade of scarlet, beside the insufficient
nonperformance, of more femoral forms pale dulcet.

By the brand or acetylene of the summer star,
or scintillation of asterisk, which aviate ember comets,
the Cimmerian screen withdraws. Unlike the louring
thunder, the water light tapering tamps, the gloriole
of morning, glister raising mantel, glare azure, upon
will-o-whist white. Pharos in every courtesy loft, the
four-de-lea of staircase cypress, passing the childish
glee of splendid Em Holden, of sconce or sun-ray
lamp, soft fragrance aids, but dalliance to veil.

Darling innocent, put to the shavings, weather's spirit in a cage,
fair and quiet in severity, white pose in the decades of tarnish,
how well the flowers fought with you, that slow age of obscurit,
tongue less silence attracted to the birds. The scold of clothing,
ornament or settling you put upon the poet, the debut of
figurant images imagined in the grass. Before these fingers moved
forward and beyond you, and you could not pull eyes anymore
form my columbine in front of you. Finally autonomous, find
coulisse in heaven, vivid alter the proscenium, bring your
versatility

Authentic bread as a woman gives, Le De'cret Pain,
Groseille sutane, the bread decree, e'pi, ear of wheat,
fruits of longanimity, Pruneax ou, parities chataignes,
fraiche, pain complet.

Petite hands of small church, mille fleur her fingers
carrying full fields, Graines de Lin, Paquetette, Aconit
de Noel, Liseron, Tournesol, gloss touch of dart, le
clocher, flambeau, autumn flan.

Flambéed pears, acreage seasons, le Demi-hectare
mascin, tea noir, femme le sucre, Pommes sechees,
Apricot sec, Pan couronne, Manqué, Baies de Goji
sechees, Canneberges. le miel, le che'ri.

My leaf of planting, Daphne or Pieris,
Hankonechloa, without the Benedick of brindle,
or frangible ground cover shivering,
fatigue of traditional graft,
seta roots more nimble,
lines vastly.
What honors brighten the wayside seed,
or talon the roots of anonymity, Bristle cone pines,
gonfanon greater hopes, uraeus seals,
to or fro Hansard wizardries
of navicert suns,
if the Dog woods fail
Plantain lilies?
Skimmia japonica, in tassels red labor,
signet governable the bitter Angelus of connote's
tiara, fictive gowns on mortarboards sold,
as married women griffon,
choice in blems of figureheads,
giving men boast inside their bodies,
fair ermine January dress,
sovereign defeated!

Machinations, to the collarbone, the crests moving,
Scouler's willows of yellow skeletons, pattern the
eleventh hour, feeling the spadework of diminished
light.

Paronomasia, piscatory, whimpering equivoque
russet seasons volte-face, diminished scaffolds, the
riddle blues of polysemy, barer trellises of massicot,
perishes celadonite, implacable odes lapis
lazuli.

The arid birds of luma are leaving, from flattened
splays of leaf lint, a long missing mistress felt in
the dust, particles of child passing through the ovoid
flowers of saucers and cups.

Piebald fall of harlequins and damascene, niello
the braille of tears sloe-black, wait May of pomelo,
currie nectarines or vermeil, intransigent orientations
of regathering habitat.

Sheep Hasht Nagri, Sheep Han, pliant of prediction,
neither mutinies of tergiversates, manageable shorn,
before takers kneeling.

Sheep Hazaragie, Gute Sheep, curations of Jacobin,
order of the breech, malleability by the lead, yieldings
of restiveness.

Katahdin sheep, Leineschaf sheep, readiness non-resistant,
for such the cabal tore down the forests, lese majesty,
obdurate infringements of mischief.

Soay, Sopravissana sheep.

Brae the wafer sol, thermotic, calcine,
liquate fuse, Celeste, obelisk, as needfire lay
flat upon aplite and I rest near Lydia stone
or serpentine, rose stones or adamants warming.
Braise olivine, dreams of Belle metal,
love be Carboly or constantan, part of tourmaline
effusifes, once of emeralds. In settings of admiralties,
vows of molybdenite, pudding stones
by psamm the grains of shore. I could bring
the lithe of leaf, but rance fail slower, sweet aventurine's.
or sultry jacinth, losses more mortal endeavors.

Phacelia flowers, Colletidae's of flitting chittarone,
purple pollens for the ramekin, thalo violet the tinctures
of sweetest honey.

Amegilla dawsoni, rehoboam sectors in Basse terre
of hives, blue pollen squills, yellow morph of sunflowers,
yellow white of heather.

Orchard bees Euglossini, carry home the brown pollen
of cherry plums, filling vacancies of tabula rasa, notes upon
truant rain, or fainting sun's of defector.

Absentees the blueish gray of borage, greens of anthers
and pannicles, greener banding lilies for pollen quilts, lost
Cretotrigona prisca who fell among amber.

Katy apple blossoms in relativities to James Grieve,
corbicula, portmanteau of the Apidae, Ashman's kernel,
carrier charms of Honey crisp and pink lady.

Esme's eyes of YlnMn blue, (in-min blue),
Agnus ribbons of excelsior, importing Sirius schisms
of light, altarpieces observing Seax cuts schematic
grasses moving, sensorial pupils of sporadic
capillary black.

Takemasa minuets, as silver censors pulse,
filaments of thermal emotion, pictorial enamels of
Pammakaristos church, brightened gold leaf of
kiln writing, Esme's black in Ottonian arts
of Meiji flames burning.

Esme's eyes of waltz permissions, tearful eidolons
recompense through met mezzanines of millefiori glass,
hope in reminiscent of Suigenkyo, pyrimaids of
incense, her lover's heart by Phoenix smoke smoldering,
craft travels of terrace time retracing.

Beginnings of Malaccan, our human weaving,
our tandem of chase braids, following umber and
beautifully evanescent diversifications of browns,
through sweet infinities of positive, negative spaces,
we rise resting artful pouches, raffia and reeding
along the exquisite ridges of grapevine, layering
soft grafts, sensual contrasts of wisteria and
bittersweet. Carrying grain between us, subtle
fragrances of wetted bowers, I know you by the
licentiousness scents of Saccharum and Themeda,
I by bromes, either by reed of moist soils, should I
entice if regent earth has made you such?

Aquarists swimmers, flexion motions Rose Dore,
fluid emotions in Thunniforms of crescent fins, hearts
in ascendant assignations or sates of Scarlet Lake.

Not as the codices or rivet stems, Countcoffe lavender,
or under-water of Davy's grey, her last of thin brushes,
Luke branches, grief of Quinacridone violet.

From the thus of Smalt seas, Phthalo turquoise as
suffer come up for air, lateral love augment false this leaf
in her river rushes, Capital Mortuum Violet.

For the runnel, the running ghyll of rillet,
dalles the apple moss which vie upon the neap,
my steps unsteady like the quavers of charivari,
on the rota of stones, I shudder sluice.

I detest in the barsat where the waters never
join, either habit of attire wherein rivers part by
callous of granite, but join the burn knavish,
by flat or gybe, the other side.

Lay the mead it's impanation, mature waters
of indecorum, where the lease of trespass seeks the
sand, Sangraal the holy beads without pleasance,
gains of prosper, ascend to rebel.

Horn rimmed tree in the meniscus prisms of the
monocle sun, henna the late day fields of grass, all ruby
shoulders in bisect of burning glass, Doric summer.

Volute reeds in blister, as tan drifts over the peach,
ochery in haruspex of lion grass, and the comb grass
as the winds portend, through reeds of broken tines.

Inchoate adit the lane of breath, something less
feasible regarding the air, what is canal to the dry
throat, as tubulus cough, from flues of Blue Herron.

Biconcave the lens of heat, subduing frocks of
Black Sapote, glare the Oak of Dodona, sufferings
zoetropes dross games of July, Sol-ish fires of

I knew the coral garden by the pacific of her eyes,
her ledge of felling by Grecian couch, the daybed
in canopy of her smile, the trundle of light retire,
the drop leaf from Winthrop's pedestal, the teaser
tissues, her borrows upon the ocean's regret.
Always unclothed despite the pleat, accouters hem
and the pearl titivate, the dishabille where the spruce
buttons are overturned and last hopes are kept, the
swivel of pearls he Stillson, her last hutch of roses,
only men possess, moieties I leave uncertain.

You made maintenance of all powers,
the heart and non participant,
a single word given, I of thousands,
inequities the singer sounds,
the tongue-less heart,
the beating dominance,
the who of love abridged by dark,
night by way of perish,
where the low chill braise upon the soil,
her mist of certitude.
Joy is the swell of timberlands,
where the birds of orchestra comment,
your silence sitting on stone,
ardency's recuse content,
peculiar beings of uneven equities,
Theron contiguous misstep,
in the end laughter sentenced over weeping,
the speaker poet mentoring,
the loneliest attritions of wordless songs.

Varying from the hemlocks
where Cochin and the nene conceal,
the redress of onion couch leave comment,
upon the snow.

I saw the flower had withered,
when she passed by,
the youth of hope had faded,
petals having turned inward,
misshapen postures peduncle,
fleet she'd become to floral crowds.
The former day had positioned her
in pride of glory, crowns of
light bent over in worship,
what kiln of moon then,
had taken from her by night,
from glean avenues or bright mezzanine?
Last winking whites of vive,
views the mists had sealed,
she passed bland by dark purples,
the hourglass pride of Ralph Shugert'
how brief an earth in practice
of garments, parcel praise
gent or lady among flowers.